Snow
CAUSES AND EFFECTS

Philip Steele

Franklin Watts
London   New York   Sydney   Toronto

© 1991 Zoe Books Limited

Devised and produced by
Zoe Books Limited
15 Worthy Lane
Winchester
Hampshire SO23 7AB
England

First published in 1991
in Great Britain by
Franklin Watts Ltd
96 Leonard Street
London EC2 4RH

First published in Australia by
Franklin Watts Australia
14 Mars Road
Lane Cove
New South Wales 2066

ISBN 0 7496 0426 3

A CIP catalogue record for this book is available from the British Library.

Printed in the United Kingdom

Design: Jan Sterling
Picture researcher: Jennifer Johnson
Illustrators: Tony Kenyon, Gecko Ltd

Photograph acknowledgements

The publishers wish to acknowledge, with thanks, the following photographic
sources:

t = top, b = bottom

Cover (centre) Liba Taylor / Hutchison Library, (outer) ZEFA / Orion Press
Title page B & C Alexander Photography, 4 Robert Harding Picture Library,
5b Robert Harding, 7b Claude Nuridsany & Marie Perennou / Science Photo
Library, 8t John Cleare Mountain Camera, 8b B & C Alexander, 9t John Cleare
Mountain Camera, 11t Colin Monteath / Mountain Camera, 13b John Cleare
Mountain Camera, 14t Simon Warner / ZEFA Picture Library, 15b Space
Frontiers / The Telegraph Colour Library, 17b John Cleare Mountain Camera,
18t John Cleare Mountain Camera, 19b John Cleare Mountain Camera, 20t B &
C Alexander, 21b John Cleare Mountain Camera, 22b B & C Alexander, 23t
Colin Monteath / Mountain Camera, 24 D Falconer/ZEFA, 25b John Cleare
Mountain Camera, 26t B & C Alexander, 28b Swedish National Tourist Office,
29t Robert Harding.

Contents

Around the world

At each end of the Earth, the planet's precious water reserves are frozen into caps of ice and snow. In the photograph, the snow-covered Antarctic is the dense white area at the bottom of the Earth. The white wisps and swirls are clouds.

Viewed from space, the planet Earth is mostly blue ocean wreathed with clouds and a white patch at each end. The white patches are the Arctic, around the North Pole, and the Antarctic, around the South Pole. They are both covered with snow and ice all year round. Although humans find it hard to live in these frozen wastes, peoples of the far north, such as the Inuit, have learned how to survive there. Not surprisingly, there are more words to describe snowy weather in the Inuit language than in any other.

In warm, tropical lands, snow is hardly ever seen except on the highest mountain peaks. These tropical lands are near the **Equator**, which is an imaginary line drawn around the middle of the Earth. In other parts of the world, people are so used to snow that they enjoy winter sports such as skiing. In North America, southern sections of South America, northern Europe and Asia, snow falls every year during the coldest months.

❊ Twenty-three per cent of the surface of the Earth is covered by snow either permanently or temporarily.

❊ Some of the world's heaviest snowstorms have been experienced on Mount Rainier, in America's Washington State. Thirty-one metres (102 ft) of snow were recorded there in the year 1971 to 1972.

❊ In 1921, 193 cm (76 in) of snow fell in one day at Silver Lake, Colorado, USA.

Skiing has become one of the most popular types of winter holiday. Every year, thousands of people visit resorts in the Alps and the Rockies to enjoy the snow.

The water cycle

Without water, there would be no life on Earth. A process called the **water cycle** gives us the water we need. The clouds covering the Earth are part of that cycle, and so is snow.

Snow falls as part of the water cycle. When snow melts, the water flows downhill towards the sea.

Water is a liquid made up of two gases, hydrogen and oxygen. It freezes at a temperature of 0˚C (32˚F) and boils at 100˚C (212˚F). When water dries out, or **evaporates**, it forms a gas known as **water vapour**.

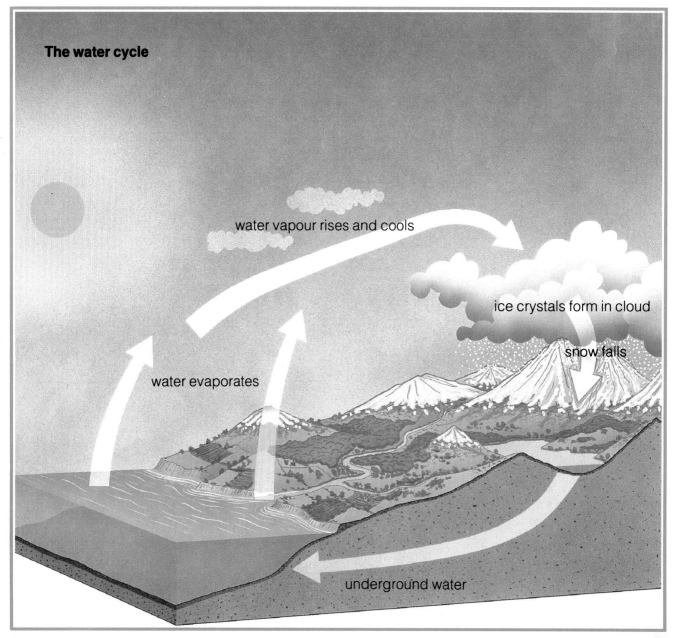

The water cycle

water vapour rises and cools

ice crystals form in cloud

snow falls

water evaporates

underground water

As the Sun shines down on the planet, it warms the oceans, rivers and lakes, and large amounts of water evaporate. The air too is warmed by the Sun and as the warm air rises it carries the water vapour upwards. The rising water vapour cools and **condenses** around specks of dust in the upper **atmosphere**. There it forms liquid droplets and it is these tiny droplets that make up clouds.

If the air is cold, droplets in the clouds may grow and fall back to Earth as **precipitation**, which includes both rain and snow. The droplets join the water cycle, falling as rain or freezing to become hail.

How a snowflake is formed

Ice crystals form in the clouds. Soon they begin to stick to each other. They become heavy and fall. If the air above the ground is warm, the ice melts and turns to rain. If it is cold, the crystals form large snowflakes.

Each snowflake is a beautiful structure built up from ice crystals, and each one is different. Some snowflakes form needles, blocks and rods. Others grow into beautiful stars. Sometimes several stick together, forming large, feathery flakes. Most snowflakes have six sides or points.

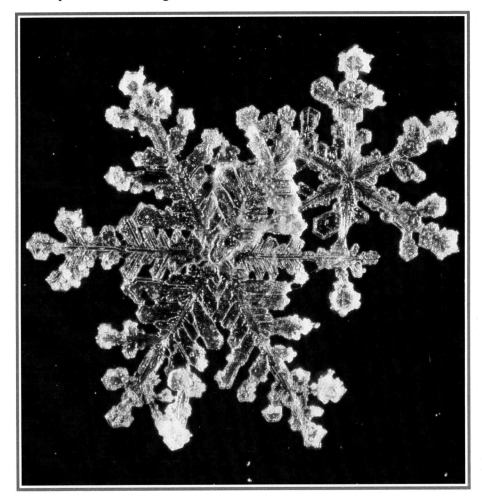

Snowy weather

It is hard to see during a blizzard. Strong gusts of wind drive thick snow onto car windscreens and into people's faces.

In spring, when the Sun shines and the temperature rises, the thaw begins. Melting snow forms streams and rivers.

Different kinds of weather conditions produce different kinds of snow. When it is *very* cold, the air has hardly any water vapour in it, and so the snow crystals are small and dry. As snow falls it can be whipped by the wind into a blinding curtain. A heavy driving snowstorm like this is a **blizzard.**

In snowy regions, it is sometimes dangerous to travel in certain low cloud conditions. Since everything is white, the horizon cannot be seen, and there are no shadows. Only dark objects show up against the whiteness. This is called a whiteout.

On the ground

When snowflakes land on cold ground, they settle. The flakes stick together and form a blanket over the soil, protecting it from the wind. If the Sun shines during the day, the snow begins to melt, or **thaw**. When it freezes again at night, the snow becomes hard and icy. If the temperature rises above freezing, the snow melts and turns to slush, and then forms puddles.

High winds can pile the snow into deep **drifts**, forming extraordinary shapes. The wind can also chill the snow until it is bitterly cold. A wind of 40 kph (25 mph) can make a temperature of -23°C (-10°F) have the same chilling effect on people, animals and birds as one of -51°C (-60°F). This is called **wind chill.**

When the snow has settled, the wind sculpts strange shapes from the snow-drifts. When the landscape is blanketed in fresh snow, sounds are muffled. Everything seems quiet.

Freezing and thawing

Next time it snows, put a small container in an open space. When it stops snowing, collect the container. Do not squash the snow down. Measure and record the depth of the snow.

Take the container indoors, and let the snow melt. How deep is the water now? Record the measurement. How does it compare with the first measurement you took?

Put the container with the melted snow in the freezer. When the water has frozen solid, take the container out and let it thaw. Measure and record the depth again. Compare your three measurements.

Seasons and climates

The weather in a particular place or country usually has a pattern over the years and this is known as its **climate**. Some parts of the world have a snowy climate all year round. Other parts of the world have seasons. Seasonal changes are caused by a tilt in the Earth as it moves around the Sun. When a part of the Earth leans away from the Sun, it becomes cold.

In mild, or **temperate** regions snow falls in the winter but not in the summer. In these regions, the air is moist and so they sometimes have heavier snowfalls than the **polar** regions where the air is dry and cold.

The polar regions are capped with great sheets of ice and permanent snow. They are cold because they are furthest from the Sun, so that the sunshine they do get has little heat in it. Much of that heat is also lost by the snow reflecting it back into space.

In this diagram the southern part of the world is tilted towards the Sun, so it is receiving more heat and light. When the Earth is tilted like this, it is winter in the northern part of the world.

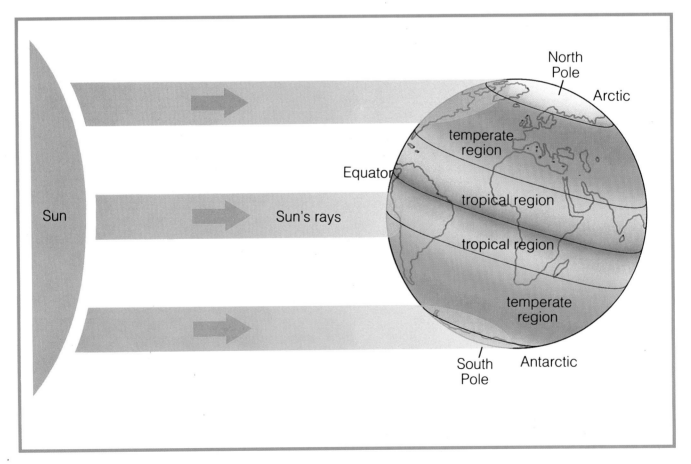

People have never lived permanently in Antarctica. Only coastal animals, such as penguins and seals, survive the harsh conditions. Today, scientists from many countries visit the Antarctic to study the climate and to measure the effects of pollution.

The Arctic is fringed by a vast area of frozen soil, or **tundra**. Most of the year it is covered in snow, but this melts during the short summer. At the opposite end of the Earth, Antarctica is known as the world's coldest continent. The temperature there hardly ever rises above freezing even in the summer months.

Snowy peaks

For every kilometre (3,280 ft) that mountains rise into the atmosphere, the temperature gets several degrees colder. Rising water vapour condenses around mountain peaks, forming clouds, and there is often a lot of snow. For example, the mountains of north-west America have a very heavy snowfall. This is because winds carry water vapour from the Pacific Ocean. As it rises over the mountains, the air cools and the water vapour turns to snow.

✳ The coldest place on Earth is Antarctica. Temperatures seldom rise above 0˚C (32˚F).

✳ The lowest temperature ever recorded was at the Vostok scientific station in Antarctica in 1983. The thermometer dropped to -89.2˚C (-127˚F)!

11

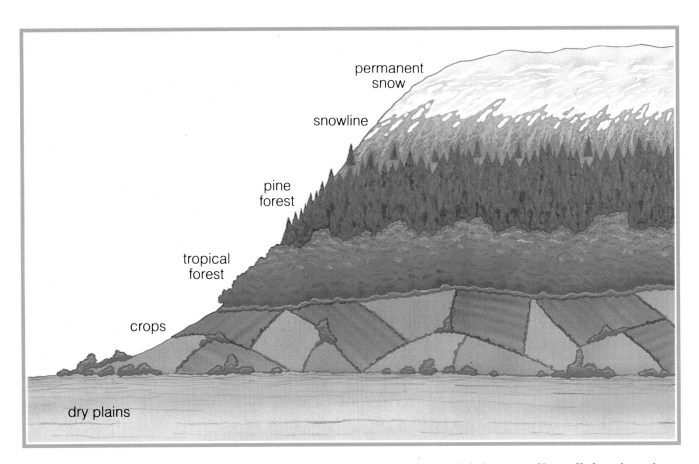

permanent
snow

snowline

pine
forest

tropical
forest

crops

dry plains

The tops of high mountains are permanently capped with snow, even when they lie on the Equator.

On a mountain, the line above which snow lies all the time is known as the **snowline**. The position of the snowline depends on both temperature and the amount of snow that falls. In polar regions, it is near sea level, and in lands near the Equator it is usually between 5000 and 6000 m (16,500 - 20,000 ft) above sea level.

Read all about it

Look for the weather report in your daily newspaper. In the winter, it lists towns around the world where it snowed the previous day. It also lists temperatures. Over a month, keep a record of snowy places and temperatures. What was the average temperature of snowy places? What was the lowest temperature of a snowy place? What was the highest?

Draw a map of the world and mark in the snowy places you have recorded. Are there more in the east than in the west? Are there more in the north than the south? Are many snowy places on the coast? Are they mostly inland, or in the mountains?

Weather signs

Both wind direction and clouds are good clues for weather watchers. Winds from the north and east can bring cold weather. Winds from the west are often full of moisture, which may turn to snow when it meets cold air. Wind patterns such as these vary. They depend on the season and the part of the world where they occur.

There are three main types of clouds. Cirrus clouds are high and feathery, and they look like that because they are formed from icy crystals. Stratus clouds lie in layers, holding a blanket of moisture. Cumulus clouds pile up in heaps, and are often seen in summer skies. Seven other types of cloud are formed from combinations of these main types. Two kinds of clouds that may bring snow are nimbo-stratus and cumulo-nimbus. Nimbo-stratus forms a dark grey or yellowish mass, and cumulo-nimbus is a towering, billowing cloud.

Dense nimbo-stratus cloud blankets the sky before a snowfall.

The winter months are risky ones for sheep farmers. In northern countries, lambs are born in late winter or early spring. New-born lambs can easily be lost in snow-drifts.

In winter, changes in wind direction or a build-up of snow clouds have always been important signals for farmers. Blizzards can cut off cattle and horses who may starve unless food can be got to them. Today many people have jobs which depend on accurate weather forecasts. Airport runways must be kept clear so that aircraft can land and take off safely. Roads and railways must be kept open. In polar regions, ship captains need to know if their ships are in danger of being trapped by ice.

Forecasts and records

Weather instruments

Anemometers measure wind speed.

Barometers measure air pressure, or how heavily the atmosphere presses down on the Earth.

Satellites send photographs of cloud and wind systems to the weather stations.

Thermometers measure temperature.

Hygrometers measure humidity, or the amount of moisture in the air.

The modern name for the science of weather studies is **meteorology**, but the science itself is far from new. The Chinese, among others, have been keeping records of the weather for thousands of years.

There are now as many as 10,000 **weather stations** all over the world, collecting data for weather reports. The information comes from meteorologists on ships and in aircraft, and from instruments in balloons and on satellites and rockets. Measurements of **air pressure**, temperature, movement and types of clouds, speed and direction of winds, **humidity** and visibility are all included.

Weather satellites are spacecraft that collect information about clouds and temperature and send back signals to Earth. Some satellites circle the Earth. They pass over the North and South Poles, and give a complete view of the Earth's weather twice every 24 hours. Others stay above a particular point on the surface of the Earth. These give a continuous view of the weather in one region.

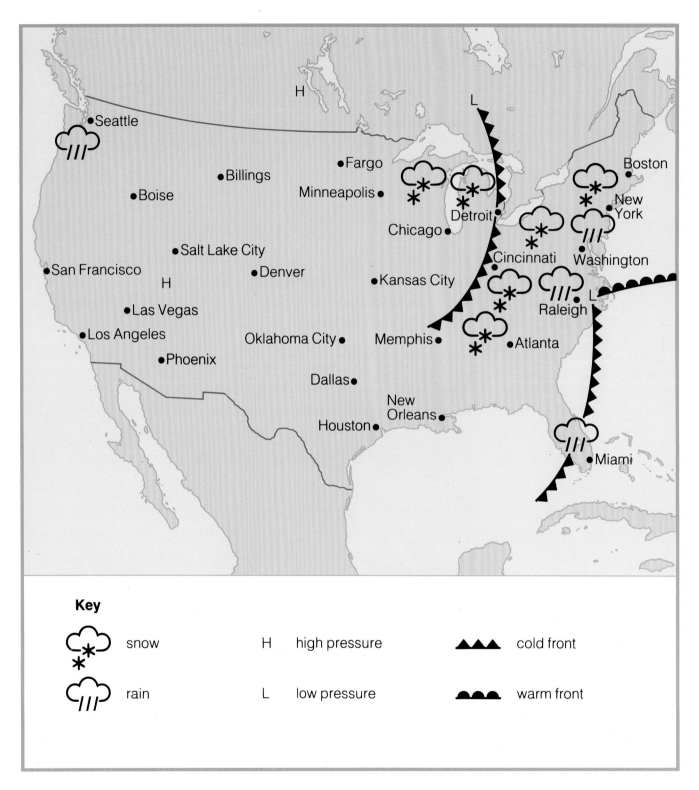

Key

⛄ snow

H high pressure

▲▲▲ cold front

☔ rain

L low pressure

●●● warm front

On this weather map snowflake symbols mark the areas where snow is expected. Areas of low and high pressure are also shown.

Meteorologists feed the information into computers that do repeated and rapid calculations. The results are used to produce the weather maps and forecasts that we see in newspapers and on television. More detailed weather maps and forecasts are issued to navigators of aircraft and ships.

Snow and landscape

The landscape of many parts of our planet has been shaped by snow and ice. Rivers of ice, or **glaciers**, have ground out deep, U-shaped valleys from the rocks in places like the European Alps, the Himalayas in Asia, and the Rocky Mountains in the USA. Glaciers are made of masses of snow pressed down over the centuries until it has become ice. They occur in high mountain areas and polar regions where more snow falls in winter than melts in summer.

The glacier in the background is gradually wearing away a deep valley between the mountains. Melting snow forms streams, waterfalls and rivers and these also wear away, or erode, the landscape.

With a great rumble, an avalanche breaks loose in the Himalayan mountains. Ice and rocks fall with the snow and destroy everything in their path. Avalanches are most common in the spring, when the snows begin to melt.

✻ Avalanches can contain over 3,000,000 cu m (105,000,000 cu ft) of snow and travel at 400 kph (240 mph).

✻ About 18,000 people were killed by avalanches in Peru in May 1970.

Danger from snow

Avalanches are a common danger on snowy mountains. Great walls of soft snow may suddenly break away and slide down a mountainside. People, animals and buildings can be buried in a few moments. Avalanches start very easily. A small change in temperature or even a loud sound can set one off. In mountain areas, people often reduce the risk of avalanches by setting off controlled explosions to dislodge loose snow.

Snow and nature

A heavy fall of snow completely changes the countryside, covering plants and grass. When snow blankets the ground, it protects both the soil and the seeds within it from chill winds. In spring, the seeds grow quickly, shoots appearing as soon as the snow melts.

On the frozen tundra of the north, spring arrives as late as June or July. As the snow melts, patches of mosses and lichen appear and provide food for herds of caribou and reindeer. In some places, wild flowers blossom even before the snow has gone.

Most conifers, like pines and firs, are evergreen trees. They have tough needles instead of broad leaves, and often have springy branches that bend instead of breaking under the weight of heavy snow.

Polar bears are well-adapted to surviving in the snowy Arctic wastes. Their thick coats protect them from the cold. They can also swim through icy waters after their favourite food of seals.

Animals in the snow

Many animals do not like cold weather. The snow covers or kills the plants they eat. Some animals have learned to move long distances in search of food before the snows arrive. They **migrate** to warmer regions.

Other animals sleep through the winter snow. Their breathing and their bodies slow down so much that they seem barely alive. This is called **hibernation**.

Snow also means that animals with dark fur can be seen clearly against the white countryside. They cannot travel far in their search for food in case they are caught by their enemies.

Some animals turn white in winter, so that they cannot be seen so easily. Stoats, hares and lemmings grow white fur, and the ptarmigan grows white feathers.

Tracks in the snow

A good covering of snow means that we can follow the movements of birds and animals. Their tracks show up very clearly. Follow a cat or dog and look carefully at the marks the animal makes in the snow. Other tracks you may find in the woods are those of birds, squirrels and rabbits.

Make a drawing of each different animal's mark you see. Measure the width and the length of each mark. Make a note of the measurements by your drawing. Keep a record of where and when you saw each track.

Can you tell if the animal was running or walking? Do you think it was looking for food?

These tracks were made by a wild cat, high in the Cairngorm Mountains of Scotland.

Snow and humans

Snowy weather means that humans must protect themselves against the cold. Even today, during a really severe winter, people still die of **hypothermia** because their body temperature drops too low for them to stay alive.

There are other dangers. **Frostbite** can damage parts of the body, such as the soft tissue of the nose, that are exposed to extreme cold. **Snow blindness** can occur when the eyes are dazzled by long exposure to the sight of white snow.

Today's polar travellers and mountaineers wear dark goggles to protect their eyes. They also wear layers of warm clothing and carry supplies of special foods to give their bodies warmth. During bad snowstorms, they stay in plastic survival bags. This is not to keep them warm, but to stop the wind carrying away their bodily moisture and causing wind chill.

The human body cannot stand up to extreme cold unless it is protected from exposure and kept warm. This Inuit hunter wears a sealskin tunic which helps to keep out the cold Arctic wind.

The traditional way of travelling across snow is by sled. The wooden sleds are pulled by teams of dogs called huskies. They are strong dogs with warm, furry coats, and can haul loads over very long distances.

Travelling over snow

Although nowadays it is possible to speed over the snow on motorised snow-bikes called skidoos, in the past snow has always made it difficult to travel far. Sleds were in use over 8000 years ago, and skis have been used in Scandinavia since the Stone Age, 20,000 years ago.

North American Indians and early American pioneers used **snow-shoes**. These were large frames, which they strapped to their feet to prevent them from sinking into soft snow-drifts. Modern mountaineers fit spikes called crampons onto their boots, to prevent them from slipping on icy slopes. They also carry ice-axes to hack steps out of hard-packed snow.

Mountain rescue

Mountain rescue teams save many lives each year. Victims of climbing accidents often have to be dug from snowdrifts or carried down the mountainside on a stretcher.

Be prepared!

If you plan to go walking in the hills or mountains, you should always be prepared for bad weather.

✳ Take warm and waterproof clothing and suitable footwear.

✳ Take emergency food rations and a flask of something warm to drink.

✳ Take a torch and a whistle in case you become injured or trapped in a snow-drift or an avalanche.

✳ Take a map and a compass, as it is easy to get lost during a blizzard.

✳ A brightly-coloured anorak will make it easier for others to spot you against the snow.

✳ Always tell other people exactly where you are going and when you expect to be back.

✳ Never go on an expedition without an experienced guide or leader.

Even in temperate lands, weekend rock-climbers and hill-walkers must be prepared for a sudden snowstorm.

In many mountain areas there are special rescue teams who are trained to search for people in the snow. Today's alpine teams have radios, helicopters, and the latest medical equipment to treat people who have been injured.

However, for centuries, dogs have been used to track people and to dig them out of snow-drifts. The most famous of the breeds used for this rescue work are St Bernards. They take their name from the monastery of St Bernard, which is on a high pass in the Alps between Switzerland and Italy. From the Middle Ages onwards the monks sent out search parties to look for travellers lost in the snow. The dogs carried a small barrel of brandy around their necks, to help revive the frozen travellers.

A snow-plough clears a road in Minnesota in the USA. Heavy snow storms can cut off small towns for days on end. Food and heating supplies have to be sent in by plane or helicopter.

Transport

In winter, heavy snow causes problems both in towns and in the countryside. **Snow-ploughs** have to be used to clear a way through drifting snow so that main roads can be kept open. Often side roads are closed to traffic because they are blocked. When passes over the Alps are closed because of snow, tunnels through the mountains take the traffic instead.

When snow is forecast, trucks sprinkle salt, sand or grit on the roads to stop the snow from settling and to give car tyres a better grip. In snowy areas, drivers put **snow chains** or special snow tyres on the wheels of their cars to stop them from skidding.

Where avalanches and snow-drifts are always a danger, roads and railways are protected from these by steel avalanche sheds. Airport runways and railway tracks have to be kept clear of snow and in some places a kind of under-surface electric blanket is used to stop snow settling.

There are other dangers from snow. Heavy snowfalls can block roads, bring down telephone lines, and create interference with radio signals, cutting people off from the outside world. Snow on the roads blanks out signposts and guiding lines. Snow-drifts can conceal rocks and other landmarks. Drivers can lose all sense of direction in a blizzard.

A pinch of salt

Salt is often placed on roads if snowy weather conditions are forecast. Why? Try this experiment.

Fill one ice-cube tray with water.

Fill another tray with water mixed with salt. Place both trays in the ice compartment of a refrigerator. Which freezes first?

Snow sports

People enjoy the snow, and winter sports such as skiing, tobogganing and bobsledding. Skiing is the most popular, and many countries that have snow regularly now have ski resorts for winter holidays. Every four years there is the Winter Olympic Games at which world-class skiers compete in a number of different events.

The world's most famous cross-country ski-race is the Vasaloppet, in Sweden. The course is 86 km (53 mi) long, and thousands of people take part.

In countries with little snow, 'dry' ski slopes made of fibre have been built so that people can learn and practise. During warm winters, some ski resorts even cover their slopes with artificial snow.

A fairy tale becomes reality at this winter festival in Japan. A glistening palace made of snow stands in the frosty air.

Building with snow

Only a few Inuit still build traditional igloos when they go on hunting trips. However, the snow houses are both warm and safe to live in. They stand up to a blizzard far better than a modern tent. Today, snow houses are sometimes built purely for pleasure. A magnificent snow palace, over 26 m (85 ft) high, was built for the 1987 Winter Festival at Asahikawa in Japan.

The children's game of building snowmen has been taken to extremes. People have constructed huge, elaborate structures from snow. One snowman built in Alaska was over 19 m (62 ft) high!

Snow and the modern world

Although snow brings problems for some, it is fun for others. Today, however, it is helping with one of the greatest concerns of our age - pollution. Cores of snow taken recently from polar regions have told scientists just when pollution of different kinds has taken place on Earth. These cores also show temperature changes over the last 160,000 years. Snow is helping scientists to understand our climate better.

Speedsters on snow

✳ Skiers can reach speeds of over 220 kph (135 mph).

✳ The world record ski-jump was one of 194 m (636 ft).

✳ In 1978, two Frenchmen skied at a height of 8200 m (26,900 ft) - on top of Mount Everest.

✳ The world's most famous toboggan course is the Cresta Run, at Saint Moritz in Switzerland.

Glossary

air pressure   The force with which the air presses down on the Earth's surface.

atmosphere   The layer of gases and dust which forms the air around a planet.

avalanche   A mass of snow which breaks loose and rushes down a mountainside.

blizzard   A violent, windy snowstorm.

climate   The weather pattern of a region.

condense   To become more dense. When vapour condenses it turns into liquid.

drift   A deep bank of snow heaped up by the wind.

Equator   An imaginary line drawn around the centre of the planet, marking the farthest points from its two poles.

evaporate   To turn into vapour.

frostbite   Damage to human skin and flesh caused by very low temperatures.

glacier   A river of snow, ice and boulders which edges its way slowly down a mountain or across a land-mass.

hibernation   A deep winter sleep. Many animals hibernate for long periods in order to stay alive. Their bodies slow down.

humidity   The amount of moisture found in the air.

hypothermia   An unusually low body temperature.

ice crystals   Patterned structures which grow as water vapour condenses and freezes.

meteorology   The scientific study of weather conditions in the air surrounding our planet.

migrate   To travel a long distance. Many birds and animals migrate in order to avoid icy winter weather or to search for food.

polar   Belonging to the regions around the North and South Poles.

precipitation   Forms in which water reaches the Earth from the atmosphere, including snow, rain, hail, dew and frost.

snow   Frozen flakes formed from water vapour in the air and made up of tiny crystals.

snow blindness   Long exposure to the glare from snow can cause inflammation of the lining of the eye. It is very painful and sufferers have to protect their eyes with dark glasses.

snow-chains   Chain belts fitted around a vehicle's tyres to help them hold the road in extreme, snowy conditions.

snowline   The line, as on a mountainside, above which snow lies all the year round.

snow-plough   A bulldozer or other heavy vehicle fitted with snow-clearing equipment.

snow-shoes   Frames made of wood and leather thongs, shaped like tennis rackets. Snow-shoes spread the weight of the body, making it easier to walk through soft snow.

temperate   Having a mild climate like the lands which lie between the tropics and the polar regions.

thaw   To melt when the weather becomes warmer.

tundra   The vast treeless plains of the far north. Deep down, the soil of the tundra remains frozen all year round. The snows melt during the short summer and allow some plants to flower.

water cycle   The endless process by which water, in the form of snow, hail or rain, falls, turns into vapour, rises, turns into droplets and falls once again.

water vapour   An invisible gas in the air . Water becomes vapour when it dries out, or evaporates.

weather station   A base for the scientific recording of weather conditions.

wind chill   The cooling effect of wind at low temperatures.

Index